THE ASCENSION OF THE PROPHETS

THE ASCENSION OF THE PROPHETS

Establishing Order In The Office Of The Prophet

Alisa Jackson

The Ascension of The Prophet

© 2020 by Alisa Jackson

Living Water Books

Christian Division of Butterfly Typeface Publishing House,

Little Rock, Arkansas 72201

ISBN 978-1-7357073-2-7

Unless otherwise notes, all scripture quotations are from the New King James Version Bible® Copyright ©1982 Used by permission.

Unless otherwise notes, all scripture quotations are from the New Living Translation Version Bible® Copyright ©1972 Used by permission.

Please note that Living Water Books of Butterfly Typeface Publishing House capitalizes certain pronouns to scripture that refers to the Father, Son, and Holy Spirit and may differ from some publisher's styles.

Butterfly Typeface

Living Water Books
John 7:38

Foreword

This book is a must-read for everyone in ministry.

It is truly a resource that will open your spiritual

understanding concerning the apostolic and prophetic.

The revelatory truth in it is outstanding, bringing forth

enlightenment and empowerment to all who are chosen

to be a voice to the nations!!!

Apostle, Dr. Tina Edwards

New Dimensions Ministries, Int'l

Memphis, TN

Table of Contents

Chapter Fourteen

They will begin to look for the prophets that have the
answer for security and provision. The posing prophets
can only promise material things, yet they are deficient
in instructions and God's timing.
The world is waiting on you, the prophet.
You are God's mouthpiece for this dispensation.

Prophetess Alisa Jackson

Preface

THE AWAKENING

Stepping out into the dawn, the light breaks forth, shining upon my face. I lift my hand to shield my eyes from the bright light, which illuminates, unlike anything I ever experienced. It showers an effervescent glow upon me and all that surrounds me.

As I step further outside the cave, the light engulfs me and lifts me to soar like the wings of an eagle. The light carries me onto the pinnacle of the mountain. There... right there, you were waiting for me. I bowed under the splendor of your glory and awaited your instructions. The sweet melody of your voice started singing, and I softly said, "Speak Lord, for your servant, hears and will obey." Suddenly, I am translated to the vision in the valley where Ezekiel and the Lord were preparing to meet. This was different from reading it; I could see the union of the prophet and our Lord.

They appeared in the valley, full of dry bones. He asked Ezekiel a very puzzling question, Son of Man, can these dry bones live?

I can only imagine what Ezekiel must have thought as he looked at the bones scattered across the valley.

- How long have these bones been here?
- How can these bones live?

He may have even assessed the previous state of the bones.

- Who were the individuals before they died?
- How did they die?

Indeed, he did not want to present these questions to God, so he gave a simple answer to the one who had all the answers.

He responded, "Oh Lord God, thou knows."

As he yielded his human intellect and accepted the frailty and limitation of his finite capabilities, he surrendered to the true and living God.

This surrender caused God to empower him in a way he never imagined. Ezekiel transcended from humanity, equipped by divinity, to do what had never been done. God instructed him to bring life back into something that carried the stench of death, no flesh, no blood, no organs, just scattered skeletons. God speaks to him and tells him something so profound, PROPHESY!

I wonder did he think to himself,
Prophesy? Lord?

There is nothing here, and the situation looks hopeless. Nevertheless, at God's command, he obeyed. Ezekiel's obedience produced an activation from the spirit realm to the natural. The earth began to yield to Heaven's authority. All that was scattered and divided became whole. Today, as I look out at the church's current state, bruised, divided, in a state of illusion, and dried up in a valley of sorts, I cannot help but hear the question ringing...

Son of Man, can these bones live?

I found my answer to be the same as Ezekiel saying, sovereign God, "Oh Lord God, thou knows." The instructions are clanging loud in my ear, Prophesy!

People ask, are prophets necessary since we now have the Holy Spirit? The answer is simple. Yes! Prophets are the church's compass that directs it to the next point of walking in the Lord's spirit and not the flesh. There is a war in the spirit realm between God's ambassadors (us) and satan, and for that reason, we will always have to fight to defeat

15

the flesh and its desires. God has become grieved with the current state of His Church. He is calling the prophets to arise and awaken His people out of complacency.

In this next level, God is commanding,

PROPHETS OF FIRE

PROPHESY!!

The Ancient Of Days

Speaks Through

Moses and An Identity Crisis

Exodus 3

11 But Moses said to God, "Who am I that I should go to Pharaoh and bring the Israelites out of Egypt?" **12** God said, "I will be with you. **14** God said to Moses, "I AM WHO I AM. This is what you are to say to the Israelites: 'I AM sent me to you.'"

Chapter One

THE IDENTITY CRISIS OF THE PROPHET

Where are the prophets? The cry for the true prophets screams throughout the land. It is ascension time, and the prophets will lead that ascension. We must take our rightful place and be the voices God-ordained. God chose us to deliver His message into the hearts of His people. We have a mandate to help steer the people of God onto the

> The Holy Spirit will closely guide the prophet into intimate relationship.

right path when they have veered off. In my earlier stages of the prophetic, I felt misplaced and conflicted. God was giving instructions of order, divine judgments, and reproaches. Yet, the prophets before were different in their response to God. I compared their actions to my assignment and lost sight of my place within the body of Christ. I did not know how to go forth or move from that position of chaos. As I attended various services, many perceived that I was a prophet, yet their understanding and perception of the calling was tainted. I wanted someone to tell me all about the prophetic, and I was expecting their knowledge of this office to teach me about myself. Nonetheless, I was having a real identity crisis. I knew I was a prophet; however, I had no idea what it entailed. I found out that the prophet's office is misunderstood and often leaves the prophet lonely. Yes, God sends the Eli's into our lives just as He sent Eli to Samuel. He sends those who have walked this path before us while also teaching us that a prophet's assignment and instructions are specific to the people that God has given them.

God wants to enter into the hearts of his people by releasing a word through the prophets.

~ Prophets Of Fire ~

The prophetic office is a place of isolation and great scrutiny. The isolation may be scary, but it is necessary because of what God needs to reveal. The Holy Spirit will closely guide the prophet into a profound and intimate relationship.

It is a partnership like none other, and your mouth becomes the portal for which Heaven speaks. I must tell you I struggled with this book because even though it is a mandate from God, I did not want to be redundant. Many books have been written, yet the prophet's office has been tainted and abused in many ways. I knew this book needed to be different, to reach the rising prophets and circumvent them from going through the struggles of many before. I honestly had personal struggles with writing this book because I tried to press past what I knew, what I didn't know, and what God needed you to know as His emerging prophet. I concluded that what I know or do not know is irrelevant.

Most importantly, I must yield to the ultimate authority - God, walk by faith and yield to the Holy Spirit. God spoke to me and told me that I could not write this book through the lens of man. The Holy Spirit knows exactly what you need to know as His prophet this season, so I removed my thinking from the equation and surrendered. You will have teachers and books to help you as you go, but the ultimate guide for you on this journey will be the Holy Spirit. He will synchronize your movements, words, and actions to His. Prophets of God are unique forerunners.

21

We are the remnant; appointed and directed by God to take the church to the next dimension. We have had many biblical examples of prophets in the bible, and I must admit that many of us would feel more lost and out of place than ever without their standard. I am thankful for their testaments and examples.

The old testament prophets revealed traits and assignments similar to what we modern-day prophets must do today. It is difficult to put a prophet in confines because their instructions are specific to their assignment. Again, I say there will be those that assist you and provide guidance along the way; even within this book's chapters, you will find wisdom, hope, instructions, and reference points. However, I need you to understand that your direct day-to-day prophetic instructions and training will come from God.

As a prophet, you are a conduit for
God's voice in the earth.
~Prophets Of Fire~

This includes submission and humility because they are essential in the prophetic.

Please understand that as a prophet, you are a conduit for God's voice in the land. Prophets reflect God's heart in the land, so it is vital to know God's voice, hear Him, and obey.

As you begin to ascend in God, you will realize your movement in God. When you walk- He is walking through you, when you speak- He is speaking through you, and when you breathe- it is Him who breathes life through you and into dry situations. It is in Him we move, we live, and have our being.

There will be times when you feel peculiar, and it is because you are according to 1 Peter 2:9. We must align our minds to the truth of God's word. *Romans 12:2 tells us not to conform to this world but be transformed by renewing our minds.*

The transformation begins when we study God's biblical truths and receive revelations from His throne. You will be questioned and ostracized by some for your words and actions; therefore, you must have an assurance that your instructions are coming directly from God.

Overcoming the Identity Crisis

Walking in the spirit is a must to overcome the identity crisis. You must be deprogrammed of the prophet's current prototype that has been presented and allow God to reprogram you. A prophet is so much more than someone who walks around pronouncing blessings and giving words. Prophets are conduits for change and shifting in the church. We are God's authority in the land assigned to guide and assist the church. The prophets know God's timing like the Sons Of Issachar and will be instrumental in shifting the church during the proper seasons of transition.

The Ancient Of Days

Speaks Through

Zechariah and The Mantle

Zechariah 1

I had a vision during the night, and there before me was a man mounted on a red horse. He was among the myrtle trees in a ravine. Behind him were red, brown, and white horses. **⁹** I asked, "What are these, my lord?" The angel who was talking with me answered, "I will show you what they are." **¹⁰** Then the man standing among the myrtle trees explained, "They are the ones the LORD has sent to go throughout the earth."

Chapter Two

YOU, CALL YOURSELF A PROPHET

Many people wear the title of prophet, but not many are true prophets. They loosely wear the title and are often misled in their belief of being a prophet because they have:

- Words of Wisdom
- Words of Knowledge
- The Gift of Prophesy

None of this qualifies a person to operate as a prophet, nor does it mean that God has chosen the individual for the prophet's office. The office is sacred, not to be entered into lightly, and no real prophet wants to be one.

I honestly must question why anyone would intentionally choose to be a prophet. I can speak for myself and tell you that being a prophet was never my desire. One of my objectives is for readers to know whether they are called to the prophet's office or have the prophetic gifting. For clarity, let's briefly look at some gifts and operations that often confuse individuals regarding their assignment. *I Corinthians 12:7-12 reads, 7 But the manifestation of the Spirit is given to every man to profit withal For to one is given by the Spirit the word of wisdom; to another the word of knowledge by the same Spirit;9 To another faith by the same Spirit; to another the gifts of healing by the same Spirit; 10 To another the working of miracles; to another prophecy; to another discerning of spirits; to another divers kind of tongues; to another the interpretation of tongues 11 But all these worketh that one and the selfsame Spirit, dividing to every man severally as he will 12 For as the body is one and hath many members, and all the members of that one body, being many, are one body: so also is Christ.*

Words of Wisdom

The words of wisdom bring clarity and instructions to the word of knowledge received from God. A word of wisdom can come in different forms, such as from someone's mouth, a vision, or a dream. Remember when Pharaoh had a dream that no one could interpret, and they called for Joseph. Joseph revealed the dream to

> *The Word of God reveals, prepares, and confirms*

28

Pharaoh, and then he came with a word of wisdom: *"And now let Pharaoh look for a discerning and wise man and put him in charge of the land of Egypt. 34 Let Pharaoh appoint commissioners over the land to take a fifth of the harvest of Egypt during the seven years of abundance. 35 They should collect all the food of these good years that are coming and store up the grain under the authority of Pharaoh, to be kept in the cities for food. 36 This food should be held in reserve for the country, to be used during the seven years of famine that will come upon Egypt, so that the country may not be ruined by the famine." Genesis 41:33-36.* In this chapter, we see an excellent example of both the words of knowledge and wisdom. Joseph brought clarity to Pharaoh by revealing the dream's meaning; he then brought insight to prepare for what was ahead. God uses the gift to provide understanding and wisdom for the present and future.

Words of Knowledge

The words of knowledge are informative words that confirm God's response in lives. The Word of God reveals, prepares, and confirms. An example is when Jesus met the woman of Samaria at the well. He reveals himself to her and equips her with the knowledge he has about her life. Let's look at the exchange between them. *John 4:18-19 states for thou hast had five husbands; and he whom thou now hast is not thy husband: in that said thou truly.* He revealed something about her current state that no stranger should have known. The woman said unto him, "Sir, I perceive that thou art a prophet."

Gift of Prophecy

The gift of prophecy is receiving a word directly from God. The Greek word for prophecy is propheteia. It means a word given by divine inspiration for reproving, admonishing the wicked, bringing comfort to those who need comfort, revealing hidden things, and foretelling future events. The gift of prophecy can rest upon one or numerous individuals at one time. It usually manifests in those who are sensitive to the flow of the Holy Spirit. One does not have to be a prophet to operate in the gift of prophecy. Individuals under the prophetic anointing or in the presence of a prophet can operate in the anointing.

Remember Saul and his men in 1 Samuel 19:20-24.[20,] *so he sent men to capture him. But when they saw a group of prophets prophesying, with Samuel standing there as their leader, the Spirit of God came on Saul's men, and they also prophesied.*

Saul was told about it, and he sent more men, and they prophesied too. Saul sent men a third time, and they also prophesied. ²² Finally, he left for Ramah and went to the great cistern at Seku. And he asked, "Where are Samuel and David? Over in Naioth at Ramah, they said. ²³ So Saul went to Naioth at Ramah. But the Spirit of God came even on him, and he walked along prophesying until he came to Naioth. He stripped off his garments, and he too prophesied in Samuel's presence. He lay naked all that day and all that night.

Therefore, people say, "Is Saul also among the prophets?" Saul and his men were by no means prophets, but because they came into the prophets' company, the spirit of prophecy was upon them. You may feel you

> Be sensitive to the flow of the Holy Spirit.

operate in these gifts, and you could be correct. Yet, you still may not be a prophet. The prophet is God's delegated vessel with divine clearance to move and exchange in the earth and spirit realm. The office carries more weight than giving a mere word and can be dangerous for anyone operating outside of God's authority. It's like a security guard trying to walk in the office of a policeman, two different authorities, with different weapons. A security guard may have a phone and a taser, while a policeman has a gun and extra security procedures. I understand that according to Apostle Paul in *1 Corinthians 14:1, prophesying is something that all should desire; however, as previously stated, the gifting alone does not make one a prophet.* As we move forward, we will look at some information to determine if you are called to the office.

In my earlier stages, God instructed me to preach and teach. I will never forget it; it was like a burning fire was upon me as God spoke to me in my room. As powerful as that moment was, He did not mention anything about the prophetic. In chapter four, *The Call*, you will learn a little more about my initial call. I use the word "initial" because I refused to accept the call after my first assignment. Prophets weren't well known at that time, and I was unsure of what being a prophet would entail. I viewed myself as unworthy, and I assumed many were more anointed than I. I continuously asked, "Why me, Lord?" I felt like David many times because I was the least among men, and everyone looked down their nose at me, wondering, how could God use her (me)?

I read of the prophets of old and their daily rejection. It seems their lives were quite a spectacle for the people, and I didn't want any parts of that kind of suffering, so I went back to doing what was comfortable and familiar, which was preaching, and teaching. I was terrified of what being a prophet would mean for my life. We were taught that there was a price for the call to ministry, but the prophetic price is even more costly. There are three aspects that one must look at before prematurely claiming the role of a prophet.

They are as follows:

- The suffering
- The pain
- The cost.

The bible tells us that Jesus learned obedience by the things he suffered. That is powerful! Our elder brother, the Son of God, taught us that suffering is a prerequisite for transformation. So, let me destroy the fallacies that the prophet's life is glamorous, that couldn't be further from the truth. Let me tell you upfront, the making of the prophet is brutal. I was born a prophet but suffered for the mantle and the anointing that comes with the office.

> Suffering in obedience to the call is a prerequisite for transformation.

Suffering is a grooming tool for the prophet. I'm not saying you will always suffer, but suffering is your training ground- broken relationships, marriages, being rejected, ostracized, on and on. I experienced it long before I even knew I was a prophet.

God was grooming me for His Glory. He was training me to understand his distinct voice and movement throughout the land. Then He used my life as the training ground. The pain associated with the life of a prophet is excruciating. I have cried so many tears of abandonment, mistreatment, broken relationships, people labeling me as strange and haughty. I have a collection of scars from my first marriage to horrible church experiences and being the black sheep of the family.

I've asked God over and over. God, why would you allow people to mistreat me? Sitting here now, I know it was all part of my grooming in becoming God's prophet. I have died and been resurrected more times than I can count. The wrestle between humanity (human nature) and divinity (spirit man) is excruciating. The cost for the oil on my life has been expensive, and in the words of the late Kathryn Kuhlman, this anointing cost me everything. The Holy Spirit trained on how to function in various atmospheres, walk in the spirit, be skillful and wage war with the enemy. Waging war consists of learning to combat the enemy's tactics, pulling down strongholds in regions and territories. Learning how to flow in the earth realm as God's mouthpiece requires much discipline and sacrifice. When others were hanging with friends and enjoying themselves, I was in solitude.

> *I was enrolled in the training camp of*
> *the Holy Spirit crucifying this flesh and*
> *you will need to enroll too*
>
> *. ~Prophets Of Fire~*

While others seemed to be advancing materialistically, around me, I was in the training camp of the Holy Spirit crucifying this flesh. I often didn't even have the luxury of telling people I was in basic training and could no longer mingle like previously. Others seemed to come and go as they pleased, dancing to the beat of their drum, but not me. I had to follow the flow of God.

There is no glitz and glamour, only submission, sacrifice, and surrendering to God to better the church, the bride. Spiritual warfare is necessary to teach you how to identify, battle, and destroy your enemy. The key is to be adequately grounded in God. Often, people try to wear a mantle that is too heavy for them. When this occurs, the mantle brings forth confusion in their lives and the body of Christ.

35

The Ancient Of Days Speaks Through

Haggai and The Position

Haggai 1

2 This is what the LORD Almighty says: "These people say, 'The time has not yet come to rebuild the LORD's house.'" **3** Then the word of the LORD came through the prophet Haggai: **4** "Is it a time for you yourselves to be living in your paneled houses, while this house remains a ruin?"

37

Chapter Three

PROPHETS GET IN POSITION

We are at a critical juncture in the body of Christ. Time seems to have stood still as we go about our day-to-day lives and religious practices. We are nowhere near our proposed destination and God's original plan for the body of Christ as a whole. As I sit back and review the events of 2020, the COVID-19 pandemic, and social injustices worldwide. The questions that rang were,

- Where is the church?
- Where are the prophets?
- Where do we go from here?

How do we get to the point of the "Greater Works" that Jesus promised? In times of great calamity, the world always looks for the children of God to show up with the answer. *John 14:12 says, "Verily, verily I say unto you, He that believeth on me, the works that I do shall he also do; and greater works than these shall he do;*

because I go unto my Father." I've heard ministers deliver great Sunday morning messages from their perspectives on the wondrous works and how we are to do them. Honestly, many have not attained *the works* that Jesus did; therefore, the greater works aren't in view. The question presented now is,

- How do we get the church back on track?

We start by going back to the basics and establishing order. Every part must be positioned and flowing as designed for the body to flow as it was created,. This leads to the second question,

- Where are the prophets?

Beginning from the days of Noah, every great move of God that has taken place was activated by a prophet of God, and this next significant move will be no different. The prophets must step into their rightful place. *Ephesians 4:11-13 [11] And he gave some, apostles; and some, prophets; and some, evangelists; and some, pastors, and teachers [12] For the perfecting of the saints, for the work of the ministry, for the edifying of the body of Christ [13] Till we all come in the unity of the faith, and the knowledge of the Son of God, unto a perfect man, unto the measure of the stature of the fullness of Christ:* One purpose of the five-fold ascension gifts is to perfect the saints in God.

The fivefold is to set the body in alignment until it models the original, Jesus Christ. Sadly, instead of modeling Jesus, we have begun modeling the world, pushing the body toward the imitator and seducer, satan. During the pandemic's beginning phases, I watched many prophets give words that did not resonate within my spirit. Some said the virus would leave as swiftly as it came. Some said it would leave after the Passover. I've seen people try to pray, fast, and even blow the virus away; however, none of these things were successful. The prophets must get into position and lead the church to victory. How can prophets lead the

> *We are not fortune tellers, giving trivial words. We are life changers breathing the Word of God into lives.*

church into victory? We lead by following the outline I have below. There are fundamental principles we must understand about the position.

What does a prophet do to get into position?

1. You must understand that you were created to effect change in your sphere of influence.

2. You are authentic. There is no one to pattern yourself after. Be ok with being different.

3. Understand you will be in the minority-generally, what you say and do will go against the majority.

4. Get into a place of real intimacy with the Father. Fine-tune your ear to God's voice and tune out the world.

5. Sacrifice is your portion. You won't be able to do what others do. You can not conform to this world; our way is the narrow path.

Please understand that positioning yourself has little to do with earthly positioning and depictions of what a prophet should be. It is a spiritual stance of authority that is allotted to a prophet to shift the church. Position your mindset to understand the actual relevance and authority of a prophet. We are not fortune tellers that go around giving people trivial words, keeping them dependent on us. We are life changers, economy shifters, world changers, and temperature regulators. If you go back and read the story of Moses and his assignment, you will see that he led the people of Israel from a time of great distress and abuse to a place of great promise. God is now positioning us prophets across the world to lead the people from pandemic to promise

The Ancient Of Days

Speaks Through

Jeremiah and Acceptance

Jeremiah 1

But the LORD said to me, "Do not say, 'I am too young.' You must go to everyone I send you to and say whatever I command you. **8** Do not be afraid of them, for I am with you and will rescue you," declares the LORD. **9** Then the LORD reached out his hand and touched my mouth and said to me, "I have put my words in your mouth.

Chapter Four

THE CALL: HE KNOWS MY NAME

Are you a prophet? Did God call you, or did man establish you? Quite the question, isn't it? I posed this question because many people are wearing the title prophet and it is extremely dangerous to run around wearing a title that God did not give you. Man can't legally ordain you into an office that Heaven hasn't authorized. You may be asking,

How do I know for sure that I am a prophet?

God told *Jeremiah before I formed thee in the belly, I knew thee, and before thou came forth out of the womb, I sanctified thee, and I ordained thee a prophet unto the nations (Jeremiah 1:5)*. Human beings cannot release the prophetic call into your life. Every prophet should have a defining moment from God where God gives a detailed account of the prophetic call.

This moment is very distinct and life-altering; the uncovering of your assignment accompanies this encounter with God. The biblical prophets had defining moments where God spoke directly to them concerning their call. It is the call that makes you aware of your earthly assignment. You were tailor-made for your assignment and your mandate must come directly from God, not man.

There are no earthly credentials that can solidify you as a prophet. *1 Peter 1:10 says; therefore, my brothers and sisters make every effort to confirm your call and election. for if you do these things, you will never stumble.* When God solidifies your call, it will be an awakening that is similar to what I like to call a Saul moment. When God called Saul to activate the apostolic mantle, which was his transformation to Paul, that moment was stellar. Reflect on the moment when God revealed your prophetic mantle to you? My moment will be forever indelibly etched in my mind because it came years ago during a very traumatic experience at a church I was attending.

While sitting in my vehicle, God pre-warned me that "they" would have to "reckon" with Him, though I wasn't quite sure of why, at the time, or who He was referring to. As I remained in my seat, that time of reckoning came sooner than I thought.

God's next instruction shook me to my core. He said, "rebuke him." I was floored and confused. You see, the spirit of religion ran rampant in this church, and rebuking an elder was a huge "No, No." God led me to the prophet, Ezekiel, to be exact, to heal me from my fleshly insecurities. I began to read and understand that the prophets had the authority to rebuke kings when instructed by God. God's instructions to me were clear, and I had to move forward. The moment for me was challenging and scary because I loved the person God instructed me to rebuke. Rebuking them was one of the hardest things I ever had to do.

Three things I knew for sure after that moment were;

1) *I was called.*
2) *I would never be the same.*
3) *This office was so much more than I could even imagine.*

The call is the initiation of the activation into the prophetic.

~Prophets Of Fire~

The Ancient Of Days

Speaks Through

Isaiah and The Purification

Isaiah 6

⁵ "Woe to me!" I cried. "I am ruined! For I am a man of unclean lips, and I live among a people of unclean lips, and my eyes have seen the King, the Lᴏʀᴅ Almighty." ⁶ Then one of the seraphim flew to me with a live coal in his hand, which he had taken with tongs from the altar. ⁷ With it, he touched my mouth and said, "See, this has touched your lips; your guilt is taken away, and your sin atoned for."

Chapter Five

THE PURIFICATION OF THE PROPHET

God is causing a fresh wind of the spirit to revive the prophetic office. There is a pureness of heart upon the chosen vessels, who are rising to their rightful places. Purity is a must for the prophets. *Blessed are the pure in heart, for they shall see God. Matthew 5:8.* Pureness produces illumination of sight into the spirit realm. Yes, I know we interpret this scripture to mean that if we are pure, we shall see God in Heaven but let us expand our thinking for a moment. When we are pure in heart it is without blemish and is defined as genuine, incorrupt, not mixed with anything. It is the condition of the heart just as God selected David because of his heart, so it is with us.

Being called is step one but contending daily with the flesh and overcoming is also a step on this journey. Before coming to God and awakening to purpose, we lived our lives consumed by fleshly

51

nature. When you become a new creature in Christ and take on His attributes, you must die to the old man daily. While answering the call of God and being filled with His Spirit has been the most fantastic experience of my life no one told me what becoming a new creation entailed. I learned that it requires the stripping of the old mentality and ideologies of the flesh. It is a complete death to self, so without the purification process and purging of the flesh, everything you do becomes contaminated.

> Holy Spirit override our fleshly desires.

Think of it like going into the kitchen, cooking a meal, and never washing your hands. Cooking with dirty hands can cause your meal to be contaminated. Purification is necessary for effectiveness in the prophetic. It require us to become naked in the presence of God and deal with personal issues head-on. We often focus on the tree (the big issues), but we must tackle the root first. The root (foundation) is what contributes to the growth of big problems. The root consists of unresolved things we harbor in our souls, such as parental concerns, rejection, broken heart, mistreatment, low self-esteem, fear, and more. We must allow God to cleanse our souls. I have learned that everything we need is in His presence.

Build an altar in your home before God and ask God to create in you a clean heart. Pray to be emptied of self and to be filled up with His Spirit.

Holy Spirit dwell within me and create in me and clean heart.

~Prophets Of Fire~

The Ancient Of Days

Speaks Through

Ezekiel and Sanctification

Ezekiel 43

23 When you have finished purifying it, offer a young bull and a ram from the flock, both without defect. **24** You are to offer them before the LORD, and the priests are to sprinkle salt on them and sacrifice them as a burnt offering to the LORD. We are now the temple of God, and our bodies are the living sacrifice.

Chapter Six

PROPHET OF GOD OR PSYCHIC

Are you a prophet of God or a psychic? According to the English Language Learners Dictionary, a psychic is defined as a person with strange mental powers and abilities (such as predicting the future, knowing what other people are thinking, or receiving messages from dead people.) As you can see, psychics "appear" to have similar gifts as a prophet, but do not be deceived; psychics gifting comes from an evil spirit. Let us look at Apostle Paul's encounter with a psychic in the book of Acts.

Once we were going to the place of prayer, we were met by a female slave who had a spirit by which she predicted the future. She earned a great deal of money for her owners by fortune-telling. She followed Paul and the rest of us, shouting, "These men are servants of the Most High God, who are telling you the way to be saved." 18

She kept this up for many days. Finally, Paul became so annoyed that he turned around and said to the spirit, "In the name of Jesus Christ, I command you to come out of her!" At that moment, the spirit left her. Acts 16:16-18.

There are a few things we can pull out of this passage of scripture; however, three stood out to me-

- She was accurate.
- This gifting was by an evil spirit.
- The gift brought her masters much gain; it was financially beneficial.

What is my point?

Accuracy does not always mean a person is working through the power of the Holy Ghost. We must follow the steps of Apostle Paul, who recognized that this spirit was unclean. 1 John 4: 1 says, do not believe every spirit but test the spirit to see whether they are from God because many false prophets have gone out into the world. This is how you can recognize the Spirit of God. Every spirit that acknowledges that Jesus has come in the flesh is from God. In the Kingdom of God, there is a

> *When someone is from God their spirit touches the deepest parts of you.*

sound. When someone is of God, their spirit touches the deepest parts of you. It is like feeling something that grabs hold of you and excites you. There is a sound, and the purification process helps to hear the sound. As I scroll through my social media, I see many that remind me of the woman that followed Paul, they are accurate, yet they have made the prophetic their gimmick and side hustle. I have seen prophets promise to give the Word of God to the audience after they have sown a seed. I attended a night service and heard a prophet say God told him there were five people in the audience to prophesy to for a $200.00 seed. I was appalled. God would never tell a prophet to sell a word. A true prophet will not charge anyone to do what God ordained them to do. *In Matthew 10:8, Jesus instructs the disciples to heal the sick, cleanse the lepers, raise the dead, cast out devils, freely ye have received, freely give.*

When prophets become like the psychics, charging for a word, how can we differentiate between the two? The prophetic gifting has endured abuse by false prophets due to laziness on the people. The distance created between some and God has caused them to chase idols. The people are pursuing prophets, and this addiction is costing them hundreds and thousands of dollars in which many may never see a return on their investment.

This type of behavior is very costly both naturally and spiritually. It pushes the prophet out of God's will. The enemy is quick to lull a person to sleep, and in hell, they lift their eyes. The love of money or greed can quickly push a prophet over the line to divination. It can quickly cause a prophet to trade loyalties from God to the devil. For clarity, let me address the question I am sure many of you are thinking. Do I believe that it is ok to have lovely homes, cars, and things? Of course, I do; however, I feel that it shouldn't come at the expense of your relationship with God or gifting.

As a worker in the vineyard, prophets should be taken care of because they are pouring out, traveling around the world, and spending time ministering to God's people. Matthew 10:9-10 Jesus also tells the disciples to *"Provide neither gold, nor silver, nor brass in your purses. Nor scrip for your journey, neither two coats, neither shoes nor yet staves: for the workman is worthy of his meat."* So, I do stand with the Word of God; the workman is worthy, but prophets must be incredibly careful by allowing the people to sow into them instead of charging. Be careful prophets, never charge for a prophecy. Keep your heart and life pure before God.

The Ancient of Days

Speaks Through

Zachariah and The Gift

Luke 1
The spirit realm became real

[11] Then an angel of the Lord appeared to him, standing at the right side of the altar of incense to tell him of his answered prayer of having a son, John the Baptist. [12] When Zechariah saw the angel, he was startled and was gripped with fear.
[21] Meanwhile, the people were waiting for Zechariah and wondering why he stayed so long in the temple. [22] When he came out, he could not speak to them. They realized he had seen a vision in the temple, for he kept making signs to them but remained unable to speak.

Chapter Seven

YOU'RE NOT CRAZY, JUST GIFTED

As I speak with emerging prophets in their beginning stages, I often hear the exact words, "I thought I was crazy." It is sad, but many have thought they were losing their minds without proper guidance from seasoned prophets. Many who are called to the prophetic see and hear things that do not appear to be "normal" by this world's standards. They are prophetic seers of the spirit realm but do not yet know how to function in that realm. Here are a couple of experiences to ponder on:

- Imagine sitting at a table speaking to someone, and suddenly you see the word liar in front of their face.
- Lying in bed sleeping, then suddenly, you hear someone screaming for help and beating on what sounds like your door, yet no one is there. Days later, news reports of a

lady found outside dead are not too far from your area.

- Some prophets experience these instances, and without someone to properly assist them in growing in the prophetic, they may feel crazy.

You see, the flesh can't truly conceive the spirit's interworking, let alone the spirit realm. Remember that in the flesh dwells no good thing (Romans 7:18). Conflicts arise between (spirit) and (flesh). So how do we overcome and ascend above the conflict between the spirit and the flesh? The power to overcome and ascend is found in our fasting and praying unto God.

What you feed most is what is
most strengthened.
~Prophets Of Fire~

In Matthews 17:19-21, when Jesus's disciples came to him wondering why they could not cast out a demon,

Jesus' response was two key things:

- They had no faith.
- This kind of depth would require prayer and fasting.

Sounds simple, doesn't it? Not entirely, you see prayer and fasting require discipline, and real discipline requires sacrifice. That is where the warring comes in, your spirit wants to yield, but your flesh doesn't immediately want to yield. Fasting and praying crucify the flesh and strengthen your spirit. The more you fast, you will begin to understand, what you thought was odd, was just the beginning of ascension in another dimension. Ascension is also understanding and flowing in the many different functions allotted in the spirit. These functions are essential to a prophet.

I would advise you to get in the spirit and stay there. The longer you are there, the more you will learn to function in that realm, and it will no longer be foreign or seem strange to you.

The Ancient Of Days

Speaks Through

Samuel and His Character

1 Samuel 13

[11] "What have you done?" asked Samuel. [12] Saul replied I felt compelled to offer the burnt offering." [13] "You have done a foolish thing," Samuel said. "You have not kept the command the LORD your God gave you; if you had, he would have established your kingdom over Israel [14] But now your kingdom will not endure; the LORD has sought out a man after his own heart and appointed him ruler of his people.

67

Chapter Eight

THE CHARACTERISTICS OF A PROPHET

Character is what produces the soundness of spirit and it separates the real from the fake. Our character is what draws the sheep further into God. In the book of Judges 16, Sampson's enemies were out to gain knowledge of the source of his strength, to destroy him. The adversary used his weakness to lure him into sin against God. I know you are thinking, "That won't happen to me." That's what many who fell before you thought too. I am sure that is what Samson felt when he laid his head in Delilah's lap; before he knew it, he turned against God. A prophet that lays his head in the lap of sin is subject to open destruction. One slip, in continued corruption, with no

> *Humility smothers pride and ushers you into your real power from the Holy Spirit*

69

repentance, and that person could easily be a vessel for satan. Let us look at some of the necessary characteristics for a prophet to have and develop.

1. Integrity

A prophet must be integral in all their ways. They must be known as a person with a strong, biblical foundation with solid moral principles. A prophet cannot be unstable, saying one thing and doing another. A prophet must live a reputable life. Often, a prophet's word is judged by his/her character because his/her word and character are one. If a prophet has no integrity, his word becomes questionable. It is challenging to receive a word of correction from any prophet, but even more difficult to accept or believe one from a prophet of dubious character.

2. Humility

Humility is the bowing down of oneself before the presence of God. The position and posture that yields his/her heart to the mouth of God and shutters at the sound that God almighty deems you worthy enough to speak oracles into your spirit. Humility is armor for the prophet, infused into the breastplate of righteousness. The fear of the Lord is the beginning of wisdom, and it is this deep reverence that we are to have embedded within us. That is the prayer of a prophet's heart, just as Isaiah Chapter 6. When he recognized he was in the presence of God, the fear of the Lord consumed him, and he saw his importance on earth shrink in the realm of the spirit while humility caused him to bow. Humility ushered him into weeping, and he released a cry, for he saw himself unclean. The fear of the Lord breathes on the trait of humility so heavily that it smothers pride. We walk upright, but we are always knelt in worship day and night, seeking God for instructions. Humility reminds us how desperately we need God and how we truly live by every word that proceeds from the mouth of God. This truth transforms us and keeps us from thinking more highly than we ought. Galatians 6:3 states, if anyone thinks they are something when they are not, they deceive themselves.

Humility must be a lifestyle due to the level of access, responsibility, and power God has entrusted to the prophet. As prophets, we are not granted the luxury of delusions of self-grandeur. We must always know and understand that we are faithful servants. A prophet must always acknowledge God as the source, and we are instruments used for the Glory of God. Humility is knowing you possess the power of free will to act out but surrendering to the sovereignty and majesty of God.

When humility is not present, we understand through scripture that two things begin to breed.

- Pride causes destruction.
  - Haughtiness causes a fall.

Pride + Haughtiness = Catastrophe. It is a deadly formula for a prophet.

Haughtiness is a bigger monster than pride; it is a false arrogance, where one believes they are superior to others. I have seen many prophets in an identity crisis that express this type of behavior. I can honestly say that at one time, I, too, possessed this characteristic. After all, I was the prophet. I looked down my nose at everyone else because being a prophet was a superior position to me. God stripped me of pride and haughtiness to teach me the true humility of a servant. Walking in pride and arrogance had me going nowhere fast, yet thinking I was on top of the world. Looking back at that old me, I can honestly say I was walking in a false arrogance.

I was still in the elementary phase of the prophetic and had no idea of my true assignment. Pride and haughtiness will have you thinking you are operating on a college level, yet you are really in pre-school. Humility is a prerequisite to ascending to the next dimension. God also wants us to operate in Love, trustworthiness, and fearlessness.

3. Love

This is the motivation of a true prophet. Love is the very essence of God, and when a man loves God, he will keep His commandments. God is love; therefore, our total motivation must be God-driven. Love propels us forward to release a message from the very heart of God to His people. It is a force that creates, heals, restores, and sustains. Love reaches out and gives the best. A prophet motivated by anything else aside from love will tend to operate from a fleshly realm and cause more harm to the body than good.

4. Trustworthy

God entrusts prophets with many mysteries and the secrets of people. This reason alone is why a prophet must be trustworthy. As a prophet, seeing and hearing from God is imperative, but even more so is the ability to keep a word until the appropriate timing is also essential.

It is an unskilled, immature prophet who goes about releasing a word before its time.

A prophet must master self-control, and self-control can be gauged by how God can trust you with what he releases to you. An oracle that is not trustworthy is like a loaded gun that fires at random. He/she will cause injury and death to many innocent bystanders. If you are wrestling with this quality, you must crucify your flesh and practice self-control to be granted clearance to the next dimension.

5. *Fearless*

Fear is a hindrance to the prophetic. As a prophet, you will have to go before leaders and people from all genres of life, and sadly not all you have to say will be excellent or favorable. I believe this is why one of the first few things God told Jeremiah was to "Be not afraid of their faces." People will often try to intimidate you when the word to them is not to their flesh's liking.

When you are God's friend, he trust
you and will confide in you.
~Prophets Of Fire

My first assignment as a prophet was brutal, so much so that the pastor threatened to put me out of the church physically. God used me to rebuke him for his whoredom, and trust me; it was not pretty.

It wasn't easy because of my love for all parties involved, and two; it was my first assignment as a prophet, and I was like a baby taking his first steps, yet my steps were sure.

Remember, God did not give us a spirit of fear, but one of power, love, and a sound mind.

The Credibility of The Prophet Must Be Restored.

For the prophets to ascend and take their vital roles in the church's stratosphere, the prophet's credibility must be restored. I have seen the prophet's character and image become reduced to nothing more than a game show host,

"Come on down...Your car is coming; your house is coming..." The ingenuine prophets are the hosts seeking to please the temporal and not the eternal for souls' sake. They shout, come on down...your car, house, and financial overflow is coming. It is a constant stream of encouragement to build earthly homes while spiritual lands are in ruins, with little investment and cultivation. I often say God will have a pure church.

Prophets must get back to the basics of the foundation to lead the church out of the wilderness.

Instead of advancing as a body, we have settled for lukewarm services with watered-down messages.

We are not allowing the Holy Spirit to transform His people's lives; however, that is about to change. The church is about to experience one of the greatest moves of God, of our times.

The Ancient Of Days Speaks Through Elijah and The Battles

1 Kings 19

10 He replied, "I have been very zealous for the LORD God Almighty. The Israelites have rejected your covenant, torn down your altars, and put your prophets to death with the sword. I am the only one left, and now they are trying to kill me too."
11 The LORD said, "Go out and stand on the mountain in the presence of the LORD, for the LORD is about to pass by."

Chapter Nine

THE BATTLES OF THE PROPHET

Each fivefold office comes with unique gifting and warfare. Battles usually come according to an individual's specific assignment, as well as ranking. It is a terrible and crushing thing to wear a prophet's title and endure a prophet's battles when you have the mantle of a teacher. Prophet battles and teacher battles are entirely different. They carry a different `ranking regarding the type of demons you will encounter and fight. Your warfare is conducive to your call and assignment. There are some spirits you must confront head-on and overcome, such as:

The weapons of our warfare are
not carnal but mighty in God.

~Prophets Of Fire~

The Spirit of Compromise

This spirit is detrimental because it can jeopardize your integrity. Compromise causes you to pervert the truth and standards you were commanded to adhere to by God, like Saul in the book of Samuel. The Greek word for compromise is *hupostello,* which means to draw in, let down, drawback, keep back, shun, or conceal. Compromise means you are rejecting (shunning) God's ways.

Remember in Matthew chapter four, Jesus fasted forty days and forty nights. After his fast, satan began taunting him, trying to get him to compromise. He offered him three options to compromise, yet each time Jesus cast him down with the Word. Your temptation can cost you your position in God. Compromising for any reason is a slap in God's face. It says to him; I do not trust you, so I'm going to do it my way. I still expect you, the one I am disregarding, to back me up in my mess.

Compromise for a prophet is especially dangerous because it affects your credibility and integrity. When a prophet begins to compromise their message, it opens the door for other spirits to come in. As I have stated previously, there is a thin line between prophetic and divination. A person with a prophetic call can begin in the purity of God, but as he/she gives into temptation, their innocence becomes compromised. The bible lets us know, there is a way that seems right to man, but its end is the way of death. I liken compromises to a brown recluse spider bite. It starts out looking like a simple bite, but it can become a gaping infected wound over days. Compromise begins small, and over time becomes a habit that infects the entire body. For example, one may say, it's ok to have a glass of wine; after all, all things are lawful but not expedient. A little wine won't hurt, then it progresses to strong alcohol; after that, it becomes full-blown alcoholism.

> Don't grieve the Holy Spirit by compromising.

The behavior begins to interfere with your integrity and effectiveness. Be sure to examine yourself to see if you possess the traits of the spirit of compromise. Do you shun the commandments of God so that you can be comfortable in your behaviors? If so, you are in a dangerous place for a prophet.

The Spirit of Rejection

This spirit of rejection can cause a prophet to become stagnate. It can take various forms, including affecting the spiritual eyesight and changing the perception of things naturally. This spirit also causes one to feel like an outcast. It attacks a person early in childhood until it gets a grip on the individual. It then continues to shape the person's life doing the following:

- **Causes internal struggles with acceptance**

The individual develops false and unhealthy relationships by choosing people who need them. Unknowingly they desire to please them and sell out for the person, hoping they will accept them.

- **Causes self-image and mental battles**

It sends the individual into an identity crisis. The person becomes so afraid of rejection that they become a chameleon and adapt to others. Losing sight of who they are. The prosperous creation God intended them to be becomes altered.

- **Causes one to operate in pride**

Rejection can cause a person to be ostentatious, desiring the spotlight, and fear losing their status.

This causes the individual to operate under a strong spirit of pride. Instead of being God's mouthpiece, they begin to adapt and twist His words to make man happy. We know this is not good because it is better to obey God than man.

- **Causes struggles with unhealthy isolation**

Isolation becomes a silent prison as the individual refuses to speak what God gives them to speak and becomes so fearful of being wrong that they never step out. The spirit of rejection is a lying deceptive spirit that seeks to keep the individual bound. Overcoming this spirit will bring forth maturity to understand that when people reject the word you deliver, they truly reject God. Another spirit that a prophet must overcome is the spirit of pride.

The Spirit of Pride

The Greek word for pride is hyperēphania, which means excessive shining or a self-exaltation that leads to self-destruction. I discuss this briefly in chapter eight as the opposite of humility; however, I expound on it more here regarding the warfare we face. Pride is a conduit for destruction, especially in the life of a prophet. It causes one to be puffed up and arrogant, taking credit for the gift that comes from God. The individual becomes haughty and untrainable because of this thinking that. they are "The Prophet." This spirit convinces the individual that they are always right and everyone else is wrong. They are like a wild bull in a china cabinet, all over the place and destroying everything that comes in their path. Pride causes God's glory to be lifted from your life, causing one to hear less and less. Ask me how I know. This spirit was once active in my life, and I begin to look down on the very people God used me to assist. I begin to be puffed up towards my leaders, and before I knew it, my gift was suppressed. The bible states that God resists the proud and gives grace to the humble. The humbler you are before God, the more grace He affords you to operate in the supernatural realm. No, God did not take my gift, but it wasn't at total capacity. Trust me when I say, though it has been many, many years since it happened, it is a moment I will never forget. The following spirit is one that all prophets encounter and learn to .

> *You are the vessel and humility is the vehicle to ride in, in order to experience Heaven on earth.*

The Spirit of Fear

The bible says perfect love casts out all tormenting fear. This spirit must be confronted and removed because fear paralyzes the prophet.

Fear is a fierce spirit that will kill you spiritually and naturally because it causes one to be concerned about men's faces instead of being focused on God. Uprooting the spirit of fear out of your life will open you to receive new revelation and expansion in the spirit. Only the love of God can bring forth deliverance in your life from this spirit.

The Spirit of Doubt

The spirit of doubt must be annihilated in your life as a prophet. Without faith, it is impossible to please God, and as a prophet, you must know who God is and know that He is for you. You must know God's voice and when He is speaking to you and through you. Why is this so important? It is important because many will question the words you speak, doubt God within you, and come against you overall on your journey. The spirit of doubt will tell you to retreat when the enemy uses naysayers to be confrontational about the word administered for the season. This spirit chisels away at your confidence, and we know the word tells us in *Hebrews 10:35 Cast not away, therefore, your confidence which hath great recompense of reward. Your confidence in your God must remain firm; thus, the spirit of doubt must be cast down.* The last spirit we are going to discuss is…

The Spirit of Religion.

I know what you are thinking. Is religion a spirit? Well, let me inform you now. It is a spirit, and it can ruin you as a prophet. The spirit of religion comes to set rules and guidelines that have absolutely nothing to do with this walk with God. Religion blocks people from seeing God and establishing a relationship with Him. As a prophet, you cannot allow religion and its man-made ideologies to shape your prophetic assignment. The spirit of religion teaches individuals to be dependent on ritualistic practices that have little to do with building a relationship with God and expanding His Kingdom. It is enslavement and requires total surrender to our sovereign God.

The Warfare of the Prophet

The prophet's warfare is not basic. A prophet has divine access to realms that most cannot access. A skilled prophet understands *Ephesians 6:12, KJV:*

"For we wrestle not against flesh and blood, but against principalities, against powers, against the rulers of the darkness of this world, against spiritual wickedness in high places. We move skillfully and strategically to tear down the works of the enemy. Prophets wrestle directly against the principalities, powers, and rulers of darkness and all their wickedness in high places. An unlearned prophet is prey for the enemy. Without skill and proper training to go among the realms and fight the enemies of darkness, you are unauthorized and unskilled, and the enemy will monopolize on your novice.

Yes, it is noble to step up to the call, but without knowledge of the weapons in your arsenal and the power and authority you possess, defeat could surely be your portion. As a prophet, you will come in direct contact with the principalities in your region that must be defeated. Look around and see what is going on in your specific region and sphere of influence.

See, pray, hear and obey
~Prophets Of Fire~

What is it?

What do you sense in your region?

Is it a spirit of perversion, division, poverty, or lack of knowledge?

Whatever "it" is, know that it is your job to confront and defeat the spirits that are devouring the people in your region as a prophet

The Ancient Of Days Speaks Through Amos and The Vital Role

Amos 3

[7] "For the Lord GOD does nothing without revealing his secret to his servants, the prophets. [8] The lion has roared; who will not fear? The Lord GOD has spoken; who can but prophesy?"

Chapter Ten

THE VITAL ROLE OF THE PROPHET

We must bring clarity to some of the duties of the prophet. After studying the ancient prophets, we know that God used them to rebuke, direct, reprove, and set order. The spiritual authority entrusted to a prophet is much greater than most realize. We have the power to shift atmospheres, regions, government, assemblies, lives, and situations. Many life experiences we encounter as prophets are symbolic. They are used to encourage and enlighten the Body of Christ. Often, prophets will experience things first to help bring clarity or show God's word in operation.

2 Timothy 2:6 "The hardworking farmer should be the first to receive a share of the crops." for example, the prophets of old had to suffer many things to show forth God's Word to Israel.

1. Hosea married a prostitute.

2. Isaiah went naked and barefoot for three years.

3. Jesus learned obedience through the things he suffered.

Suffering produces a great harvest. We must understand that our suffering produces fruit far beyond our comprehension, which will allow us to assist in building, shifting, and activating the church Activation is stirring up the gift which appears in scripture *2 Timothy 1:6 Therefore, I remind you to stir up the gift of God, which is in you by the laying on of my hands.* Activation is used to ignite believers to go forth in various levels of their assignments. This is something a prophet must take very seriously and commit to the task carefully.

Activation out of season could be detrimental to that individual. Some of the ways prophet change atmospheres are through,

Spoken Word

God's word is alive and on assignment. He releases expedient words to share with the body. When prophets speak to individuals, churches, regions, nations, the word becomes like electricity that spreads, producing power everywhere.

Prophets of fire coming forth will be that spark that spreads and catches a nation on fire for God,

Prophetic Prayers

These are prayers that come directly from the heart of God that activate the people of God, causing a significant shift. When Jesus taught the disciples to pray, He established a prayer pattern that shifted and prepared to beckon Heaven and receive a response.

Prophetic Songs and Worship Dance

Often called prophetic worship, these are Rhema words through songs and movement. Each song or dance is an offering unto God inspired by God through the Holy Spirit. God moves among us just like lightning dances through the skies and flashes a bright light. God delivers his sound through movement.

Imparting the Mysteries of Heaven

Prophets who walk in spirit receive access to the mysteries of God. There must be an openness to the promises of God beyond what is on the pages because it is alive and limitless. Now please understand, I am not admonishing you to go outside of the bible but travel more in-depth within the presence of God. Allow the Word to expand within you to receive the mysteries of God.

Colossians 1:25-26, ²⁵ I have become its servant by the commission God gave me to present to you the word of God in its fullness— ²⁶ the mystery that has been kept hidden for ages and generations but is now disclosed to the Lord's people.

Ephesians 3:7-11 ⁷ I became a servant of this gospel by the gift of God's grace given me through the working of his power. ⁸ Although I am less than the least of all the Lord's people, this grace was given me: to preach to the Gentiles the boundless riches of Christ, ⁹ and to make plain to everyone the administration of this mystery, which for ages past was kept hidden in God, who created all things. ¹⁰ he intended that now, through the church, the manifold wisdom of God should be made known to the rulers and authorities in the heavenly realms, ¹¹ according to his eternal purpose that he accomplished in Christ Jesus our Lord.

In these passages of scripture, we see the truth of God's mysteries; things that once were veiled from man have now become accessible through Jesus Christ. The secrets of God are birthed through His word, by the Holy Spirit.

I must say that entering the first dimensions. One may be like a newborn calf trying to stand for the first time, a little shaky and unstable. However, the higher you ascend, the more these necessary characteristics are developed. Notice that I said developed, not created, which means they are present in you. The more you avail yourself to God, the more he entrusts you. When there is an openness to God and his living word, our sphere of access enlarges. We began to comprehend the things of God more than earthly things. There are points of entry we ascend to beyond this physical realm. As prophets, you must understand that though you are in the world, you are not of the world. In John 17:16, Jesus made a compelling statement in His prayer for the disciples, "They are not of the world, even as I am not of the world." We know well how to function in the physical realm, the seen realm. However, little is known about the heavenly realms and how we are to operate in these realms. As a prophet, you must acclimate yourself to the heavenly realm. It must be just as familiar to you as the physical realm because this is your true sphere of existence. You are not of this world.

> It's time to comprehend the things of God.

95

It is time for you to conform to your true origin, Heaven. What you feed most is what you strengthen the most. The more you begin to crucify the flesh, the more you build up your spirit man and have access to other realms and dimensions. I can't imagine the cost the ancient prophets had to pay for the level of access they experienced in other realms and dimensions.

For instance, in his writing of Revelations, John was in exile on the Isle of Patmos when he received the grand vision of the end times. During loneliness, loss, and discomfort, God granted John access to hidden mysteries, and secrets of the time were revealed to him. Can you imagine the splendor that he beheld? *"12 I turned around to see the voice that was speaking to me. And when I turned, I saw seven golden lampstands, 13 and among the lampstands was someone like a son of man, dressed in a robe reaching down to his feet and with a golden sash around his chest. 14 The hair on his head was white like wool, as white as snow and his eyes were like blazing fire. 15 His feet were like bronze glowing in a furnace, and his voice was like the sound of rushing waters. 16 In his right hand, he held seven stars, and coming out of his mouth was a sharp, double-edged sword. His face was like the sun shining in all its brilliance." Revelation 1:12-16*

Many have not experienced this level of revelation because of:

1. The lack of pursuit of God. Many do not pursue God beyond vain prayers and religious practices.

2. Ignorance- many will read John's account in Revelation and think that level of access is not attainable to them. The bible informs us that if we seek, we will find.

3. Not wanting to die. Many want to remain comfortable in their flesh, to enjoy the fleshly benefits.

4. Fear- Many fears that this type of revelation will bring the rejection of man, leading to exile and ostracizing. I will concede that there could be some truth to this thought. However, you were sent with purpose, and it must be fulfilled. Ostracizing and rejection are inevitable for the authentic prophet. The bible warns us, "Woe unto you when all men speak good of you." Why is this? If all men are speaking good of you, then that means you must be doing a lot of people-pleasing and not God-pleasing.

Prophetic Dispensations and Seasons

What is a dispensation? A dispensation is defined as natural realms and spiritual realms.

natural realm: 1.) The divine ordering of the affairs of the world. Spirit Realm 2.) An appointment, arrangement, or favor, as by God. 3.) A divinely appointed order of age. I refer to these moments as divine appointments with destiny that are irreversible or unavoidable. A divine appointment is a place where Heaven invades earth. When we look throughout our bibles, we see two things, 1.) Every significant move of God in the bible was a changing of dispensations. 2.) God used a prophet to initiate and lead change.

Just think about it, if we look back to Noah, we will see that the whole earth was destroyed, and God started over. If you look at Moses's story, we see he came along when God's people were in great slavery and oppression. Moses initiated and helped lead the people to their next dispensation.

In the 1900s, God used a man named William J. Seymour to jump-start revival, known as the Azusa Street revival. This was the beginning of a new dispensation. The next divine appointment will be a culmination of moves that will connect believers everywhere. Will you be the Noah, the Moses, the William of your time?

I hear the cry of God, "Let my people go!"

It is time for a great move of God to release His people from the enemy's bondage and deceptions. It is your time, Prophet! No longer can you sit in the background making excuses. When God called Moses, he had excuses, too, one being his speech.

- Maybe you are not an eloquent speaker.
- Maybe you can't quote every scripture to the exact word.
- Perhaps you don't feel you look the part; you feel too old, too young.

Whatever the excuse may be, it is time to lay it down at the altar and pick up your marching orders. Rather you like it or not, whether you understand it or not. You may not have a significant role like Moses, but you are uniquely designed for your assignment as a prophet.

God will begin to stir your spirit. He will begin to shake you and snatch you out of complacency. One thing you must know is that His word will not return to Him void. It is time for you to arise, great prophet; this dispensation is your responsibility.

There are several distinct great dispensations throughout time and a multiplicity of seasons. God's seasons are not like man's seasons confined to the five seasons based on weather/climate change.

Each season initiates something different within the body of Christ. Our job is to make the church aware of the access and activities taking place in various realms. We are all familiar with Ecclesiastes 3, but let us dig a little deeper into the complexity of seasons. *Ecclesiastes 3:1-8, 1 There is a time for everything, and a season for every activity under the heavens: 2 a time to be born and a time to die, a time to plant and a time to uproot, 3 a time to kill and a time to heal, a time to tear down and a time to build, 4 a time to weep and a time to laugh, a time to mourn and a time to dance, 5 a time to scatter stones and a time to gather them, a time to embrace and a time to refrain from embracing, 6 time to search and a time to give up, a time to keep and a time to throw away, 7 a time to tear and a time to mend, a time to be silent and a time to speak, 8 a time to love and a time to hate, a time for war and a time for peace.*

The scripture above lets us know there is a season for every activity under the heavens. Have you ever seen times when there are large amounts of births in the land? You must realize what is happening in the natural is happening in the spiritual realm. It is also a birthing season in the spirit realm, birthing dreams, visions, ministries, even a "new" you.

As I am writing this chapter, we sit in a multi-season—a season of growth, prosperity, and sadly great death. People are experiencing growth in multiple ways while in the pandemic. We are experiencing prosperity like never before, business ideas are being born, and sadly, death is at an all-time high in the natural. Yes, many things are happening at once in this season.

Remember, in God, timing is entirely different, and so are His seasons. I believe this is the reason we see a lot of discontentment in the church regarding prayer requests because we are expecting Him to show up according to our schedule. The bible lets us know a thousand years is like a day to God. God uses His prophets to declare the season for the church. We are to discern the "climate" for the body of Christ and alert them to the activity of the seasons. Prophets are usually the first to discern the change in seasons so that they may effectively instruct the body of Christ into each open season. When I think of an open season, I think about the man sitting by the side of Bethesda's pool. *Now there is in Jerusalem by the Sheep Gate a pool, which is called in Hebrew, [a]Bethesda, having five porches ³ In these lay a great multitude of sick*

> You are the chosen one for this next dispensation

people, blind, lame, [b]paralyzed, [c]waiting for the moving of the water. [4] For an angel went down at a certain time into the pool and stirred up the water; then whoever stepped in first, after the stirring of the water, was made well of whatever disease he had. John 5:2-4

It is imperative to move quickly during open seasons; for a prophet, it could be life or death. There are many seasons in a prophet's life.

- **Seasons of silence**

  These seasons are where God is downloading into your spirit, and you aren't speaking a lot. Sometimes it also seems as though God is not speaking to you. At these times, the downloads from Heaven are beyond human comprehension; it's all spiritual. During these seasons, you will "feel" like you are supposed to be busy prophesying. You will feel out of place. Rebuke the antsy spirit and command your spirit to settle in as God continues to download, read, study, spend moments in intense prayer (remember prayer is a dialogue)

- **Seasons of The Cave**

  Cave seasons are necessary for a prophet. Those cave moments give prophets their second wind and increases hearing God in a way they never have before. Cave experiences seem like you are having a pity party. These are times when you feel so awkward and all alone. You may even question your mantle and call during these times. Be sure to take courage. Nothing is as it seems. God has you isolated for your next assignment.

- ## Seasons of Great Revelation

  These moments are generally after the cave or potter's wheel season. After spending some much-needed time in solitude and intimacy with God, you will come out with instructions from God, just as Moses did.

- ## Wailing Season

  This is a time of ample warning and instruction to the church. This is a tough season for many prophets because it is one of rebuke, warning, and correction for the body of Christ. Stand firm in this season; don't give up or give in. No one likes correction; however, every child should humbly accept correction, even you prophet, we must all understand that God chastens those He loves.

- ## Season on The Potter's wheel

  This is where it seems God is making you all over again, fitting you for your new assignment. This one seems particularly difficult because it feels like you are spinning and unsure which way to go next. In this season, "Stay on the wheel!" allow God to transform you. Don't be anxious for an answer. Just be still and let God hold on to you and shape you as He sees fit.

How you handle and conduct yourself as a prophet in each season determines your next level or promotions granted.

The Ancient of Days Speaks Through John The Baptist and Leading Men to Christ

John 1

26 "I baptize with[e] water," John replied, "but among you stands one you do not know. **27** He is the one who comes after me, the straps of whose sandals I am not worthy to untie." **29** The next day, John saw Jesus coming toward him and said, "Look, the Lamb of God, who takes away the sin of the world! **30** This is the one I meant when I said, 'A man who comes after me has surpassed me because he was before me.'

Chapter Eleven

PROPHETS DON'T BECOME AN IDOL

As a prophet, it is of the utmost importance that you always walk in humility and lead the people to God, not you. Some prophets teach people dependency on them instead of teaching them how to build a relationship with God. When a prophet becomes puffed up for earthly gain, they become in danger of being like Lucifer, who was kicked out of Heaven due to his pride. *12 How you have fallen from Heaven, morning star, son of the dawn! You have been cast down to the earth, you who once laid low the nations!*

> God is a jealousy God. He shall have no other God before him.

13 You said in your heart, I will ascend to the heavens; I will raise my throne above the stars of God; I will sit enthroned on the mount of assembly, on the utmost heights of Mount Zaphon. 14 I will ascend above the tops

of the clouds; I will make myself like the Most High."
Isaiah 14:12-14

Desiring earthly gain is prideful, and the spirit of pride combined with the anxious spirit in the land produces ungodly results. In this microwave generation, we want everything quickly, including an answer from God. People don't want to put in the work to mature their spirit man and increase their ability to hear God for themselves. People want revelation without a relationship, and this is an error. I've seen people run to get a word from prophets rather than seeking God directly. The people have become gluttonous for the prophet's words and are famished from direct words from God. Many turned from prophets of God to false prophets in divination, so instead of drawing individuals closer to God, they are pulling souls further away, luring them into the enemy's territory. People are unknowingly being bewitched by the enemy because they desire a "quick" fix more than God.

Desire God more than anything and anyone. ~Prophets Of Fire~

The Ancient Of Days

Speaks Through

The Two Witnesses

Revelations 11

[3] And I will appoint my two witnesses, and they will prophesy for 1,260 days, clothed in sackcloth." [5] If anyone tries to harm them, fire comes from their mouths and devours their enemies. This is how anyone who wants to harm them must die. [6] They have the power to shut up the heavens so that it will not rain during the time they are prophesying, and they have the power to turn the waters into blood and strike the earth with every kind of plague as often as they want.

.

Chapter Twelve

PARTNERSHIP
THE APOSTLE AND PROPHET

In the Book of Revelation, chapter eleven, there's a partnership between two witnesses. Some versions mention that they are prophets; other versions say, two witnesses. However, the authority and power they have are not only prophetic but also apostolic. I used the scripture to begin this chapter because God ordained them as two olive trees and two lampstands standing before God. The bible states that fire proceeds from their mouths to destroy their enemies. God gave them the power to shut up Heaven, turn water into blood, and strike the earth with all kinds of plagues. As I continued to read, this partnership didn't just reign together in the glorious

> God has given us the power to shut up heaven and turn water into blood.

111

times; no, they endured war together. The beast made war against them and, for a time, overcame them. I imagine these are the moments in life that seem unbearable for both offices..

These two witnesses died together. They were strong and mighty together even in their spiritual and natural death. This reminded me of the times when apostolic and prophetic will sometimes endure hard seasons but still must remember how powerful they are together. After facing hardship, we witnessed the resurrection power that rested upon these two after they experienced a three-day death. It was the very breath of God that entered them and placed them on their feet. Heaven told them to ARISE, come up here. They ascended together on a cloud into Heaven. The partnership of two joining together is symbolic here. *11 So Christ himself gave the apostles, the prophets, the evangelists, the pastors, and teachers, 12 to equip his people for works of service, so that the body of Christ may be built up 13 until we all reach unity in the faith and the knowledge of the Son of God and become mature, attaining to the whole measure of the fullness of Christ. Ephesians 4:11-13.* Christ gave apostles and prophets the power to equip his people for service works until we all reach unity in the faith and the knowledge of the Son of God and become mature.

The word unity stands out for me regarding this partnership. The apostle and prophet's office can look similar; and for this reason, many operate in an identity crisis when it comes to the two offices. We often emphasize how the prophet is ordained before being formed in his/her mother's womb, but so was the apostle. Saul's conversion to Paul wasn't something that just happened. The ordination took place before the foundation of the earth to lead the church into a new era. Such as it was then, so it is now. God is aligning his apostles and prophets for a mighty shift in the church. We are all one body but many members. We all represent parts of this body that represents the bride of Christ.

Apostles Are The Hands of God Establishing With The Heart Of God

They are sent to build, establish, govern churches, and regions throughout the government of God. Apostles equip the body with sound doctrine as they build on Christ's foundation in the church. God instructs apostles to assist everyone in natural and spiritual development. Apostles build disciples for the great commission of Christ, and they equip the saints.

In Titus 1:1, Paul writes," Paul, *a servant of God and an apostle of Jesus Christ to further the faith of*

113

God's elect and their knowledge of the truth that leads to godliness."

Prophets Are The Mouthpiece Of God, Speaking The Heart Of God

We are not only graced to hear and see, but to speak, instruct, direct, and lead God's body. The apostolic and prophetic have a weighty assignment, and it is easy to see how the offices connect to assist one another. Can an apostle function without a prophet in the house? Definitely! Can a prophet function without an apostle? Definitely! However, the two offices' are necessary for the church to grow and flourish as God intended.

> *A partnership built in Christ that is necessary for the church to flourish in God*

The partnership can be described as God impregnates the apostleship. The apostle gives birth and nourishes the child, while the prophet guides the child. The prophet helps the apostle shift the body to the next dimension. There have been instances where apostles and prophets face severe attacks amongst one another, just as Revelation 11 gives insight to the war that the two witnesses face together. These attacks hinder the partnership when the two don't have a clear understanding of what is occurring, if each refuse to humble themselves and join to help one another. I have listed several hindrances below for the use of training.

Attacks That Hinder The Partnership

- When prophets don't fully understand the office's function and the apostle doesn't discern the prophet's calling, they can become misplaced at local assemblies. This misplacement can cause chaos.

- When an apostle doesn't understand the prophet's assignment or the importance of the prophetic flow in the services, this stifles the prophet's growth and grieves the Holy Spirit.

- When a prophet has a haughty and prideful spirit, this interferes with the relationship. The apostle may receive instructions from God to refuse the prophet's services for a season, and this decision can place a barrier between them due to the prophet's lack of understanding.

- Denied access from an apostle can limit the functionality of the prophet, causing stagnation in the body. Without the apostle releasing the prophet to flow prophetically, the prophet is restricted and limited in assisting the church. Complacency hinders the movement of God in the partnership.

- When a spirit of witchcraft is present, the apostle will begin operating in division, thinking that if a prophet is released, the members' loyalty will be divided. This corrupt behavior

115

weakens the body and leaves both the apostle and the prophet wounded. The truth is both offices are leadership roles, and they must understand their positions as it relates to a local assembly. Like a president and vice president who have different functions, yet each is a necessity.

While this list doesn't cover everything, it is used as a teaching tool to inform and educate on how clever satan can be in his attempt to steer us away from God and one another. Developing the bond between the apostle and prophets is beneficial to the church for several reasons.

The Benefits Of The Partnership

- Christ is the chief cornerstone. He is the foundation every apostle and prophet build on. Under the Holy Spirit's tutelage, we provide stability and guidance to the local assembly and community.

- Together we are perfecting and strengthening the body. In the Book of Acts, when clarity and instructions were needed for Antioch's church, the apostles and elders' council sent Paul and Barnabas, Apostles, along with Judas and Silas; Prophets (Acts 15:32). All four delivered the letter. Judas and Silas spoke words of encouragement and strength to the church and returned home. Paul and Barnabas remained with the church and taught and preached the Word of The Lord.

- Each office had a distinct role to play in the growth of the church. Prophets generally flow prophetically and

116

encourage the body, and the apostles teach and direct the body of Christ.

- Together we build. The church must be fully built up and complete in every area.

Each position comes with authority and grace, which is a force to be reckoned with when combined. It is time for both offices to do their parts to break down all barriers hindering the full collaboration of the offices. The apostles must confidently allow the prophets to function fully, and the prophet must go forth in humility and boldness. When these two offices come together and become a solid foundation, the church will be unstoppable. I have combined a list of strength that makes this partnership prosperous in Christ.

The partnership of the apostle and the prophet should contain understanding, relationship, mutual respect, communication, humility, and balance.

See a breakdown below of these areas.

- **Understanding:**
  There must be a complete understanding of each office's function and what it will take for both to accomplish what they were sent to the earth to do.

- **Relationship:**

  The offices can't work together without a common bond, which generally starts with Christ and the church. They don't have to be best friends, but there should be a camaraderie between the two.

- **Mutual respect:**

  There must be mutual respect as individuals and in the offices. It is almost impossible to work with someone you don't respect. When both respect the other, the relationship is reciprocal.

- **Communication:**

  Open communication is key to working together for the growth of the church. Both parties must come together and be able to discuss things in their hearts.

- **Humility:**

  There can be no pride and arrogance when collaborating for the growth of the church. Prophets must understand that they are present to assist, not to take over or to lead. The apostles must understand their role and not be intimidated by the flow of the prophet.

- **Balance:**

  The offices should balance one another out and support one another in prayer, fasting, words of encouragement, and direction.

The apostle and prophet must understand that there is only one agenda that needs to go forth, and that's the agenda of Jesus Christ. *Ephesians 4:2-7 "with all humility and gentleness, with patience, bearing with one another in love, making every effort to keep the unity of The Spirit through the bond of peace. There is one body and one Spirit, just as you were called to one hope at your calling, one Lord, one faith, one baptism, one God and Father of all, who is above all and through all and in all*

The Ancient Of Days

Speaks Through

Jesus and The Crucifixion of Flesh

Matthew 26

38 Then He *said to them, "My soul is deeply grieved, to the point of death; remain here and keep watch with Me." 39 And He went a little beyond them, and fell on His face and prayed, saying, "My Father, if it is possible, let this cup pass from Me; yet not as I will, but as You will."

121

Chapter Thirteen

THE PLACE OF THE SKULL - GOLGOTHA

We have all heard theologians expound on the scripture concerning the death of Christ, and it is impossible to expound on the death without stopping by Calvary, also known as Golgotha. Golgotha in Latin means bald head or skull. It is the location of the crucifixion of our beloved Christ.

The place of the skull was a place of dying that was greater than natural death. Remember in the Garden of Gethsemane, Jesus prayed, My Father, if it is possible, may this cup be taken away from me; Yet not as I will, but as you will." Jesus felt great distress in the flesh, thinking about what He had to face. He prayed fervently for another way, some way to escape the bitter cup before Him.

He knew what He was sent to accomplish, but at that moment, He didn't want to do it, so He cried out to His Father. Jesus' prayer was a pivotal moment, a wrestle of wills; the success of Jesus's mission depended on Jesus's yielding in prayer. He prayed with reverence, and HIS request was granted. Remember Jesus was the lamb slain before the foundations of the world, meaning He agreed to the coming sacrifice for us all. Now think about what God has asked you to do. Have you agreed to it? No matter how difficult or challenging it is, what people have to say about what God has asked you to do doesn't matter? Peter said I'd rather please God than men. We often focus on this request as a point of discussion but what came after was the most powerful.

I'd rather please God than men.
~Prophets Of Fire~

Jesus stated, "Nevertheless not my will, but Thine be done." After this powerful statement, an angel appeared to Him and strengthened Him. We can only imagine the battles that Christ endured at the place of the skull. Reading the scripture, we know that it was an intense and excruciating physical torment, but we must also understand the battle emotionally and mentally.

God is a purposeful God, and we must know that the crucifixion taking place at the place of the "skull" is no accident. Imagine the mental anguish that Jesus endured. He was wrestling with humanity and divinity for greater accessibility and power. He wrestled for the lost. He took undeniable cruelty so that all could be saved, and yet there was a point when he cried out, "My God, My God, why has thou forsaken me?" When Jesus released this cry, he was separated from that which he had always known *2 Corinthians 5:21 lets us know that He made Him who knew no sin to be sin on our behalf so that we might become the righteousness of God in Him.* Scholars will teach that because God could not look upon the sin upon Jesus, He turned His back, and there was a separation. At the place of the skull, Jesus went through the greatest battle of his life mentally, emotionally, and physically. This is what he was born for; he was created for something bigger than himself, and his battle would open a door that many could walkthrough for ages.

> We wrestle against humanity and divinity.

- How does this connect with the prophet's office, and why must each prophet visit the place of Golgotha?

125

A prophet must come to the place of dying to self. In scripture, Paul writes, *"I die daily..."*, A prophet must come to the end of themselves. There will be a place of wrestling between humanity and divinity, a wrestle between what seems rational and truly God. I must warn you that this wrestle will cost you.

It will cost you because it will require that you genuinely transcend into the spirit realm and walk in the spirit on another level. This will cause you to go from what you "believe" to be true to what is. God will allow you access to what you never knew existed. Acceptance of the call involves coming to a place of total surrender.

The eyes of your understanding become enlightened. You will understand how peculiar, gifted, and destiny driven you are. You will realize there is only one way out, and that is to go through. At this point, with all the realizations, something unique will happen. You will stop kicking against the current, lie on your back, and float.

Simply put, you will stop wrestling in your mind and die to self, to access a level of the spirit in dimensions you never knew existed. You will finally go from being ordinary to extraordinary. You will then walk as God's prophet on the earth.

The Ancient Of Days

Speaks Through

Elisha and The Ascension

2 Kings 2

When they had crossed, Elijah said to Elisha, "Tell me, what can I do for you before I am taken from you?" "Let me inherit a double portion of your spirit," Elisha replied. **10** "You have asked a difficult thing," Elijah said, "yet if you see me when I am taken from you, it will be yours—otherwise, it will not." **11** As they were walking along and talking together, suddenly a chariot of fire and horses of fire appeared and separated the two of them, and Elijah went up to Heaven in a whirlwind. **12** Elisha saw this and cried out, "My Father! My Father! The chariots and horsemen of Israel!" And Elisha saw him no more. Then he took hold of his garment and tore it in two.

127

Chapter Fourteen

PROPHET ASCEND

After death, there's ascension...

When I look at the church's current state, it brings tears to my eyes, and I know they are the tears of our Father for His bride's condition. He entrusted His precious possession to us, and many have made a mockery of it and left it as the Samaritan on the side of the road, bloody, beaten, stripped, and abandoned. God is about to resuscitate the church and breathe His breath, RUAH, into the church again.

This reviving will call forth a rising of the true prophets. I believe there is a calling from the four corners of the earth for prophets to arise together.

Releasing The Clarion Call

Prophet,

I command an awakening in your spirit even now. I snatch you out of the cave and the low places you have been in and cause you to arise.

No more confusion!

No more role reversal!

No more wondering!

No more playing church!

It is time for the Ecclesia to rise, rule, and reign, walking in absolute kingdom authority. They that know their God shall be strong and do exploits. Exploits are defined as bold and daring feats. Those that know God will boldly make full use of the authority allotted to them. If we are not doing exploits, we can only surmise that we do not know God. We know of God.

I know some would seek to argue with this observation, but only from the basis of the natural, which indeed has no absolute precedence when dealing with matters of the kingdom. We must remember that the kingdom is not meat and drink. These tangible things we see daily.

The kingdom is spirit. It is alive with great power and authority, and the church has yet to transcend to true kingdom rule. Christ gave the blueprint, "Thy Kingdom come; thy will be done in earth, as it is in heaven..." "Come Kingdom, Come Kingdom!!!" I adjure the kingdom is about to be unveiled in one of the most incredible ways ever, and for this unveiling, the prophets must get in position to lift the veil.

The kingdom is not tangible

things we see every day.

Heaven is within you and I.

~Prophets Of Fire~

Epilogue

In 2019 I began writing this book, afraid and unsure of where to contribute to this era's prophets. I quickly realized my worries were trite, fueled by a human perspective. The deeper I went in writing, the more I realized I wasn't writing the book at all. It was through the inspiration of the Holy Spirit the writing was flowing. I realized God was doing what He has always done with His prophets, sending instructions for what's to come. The difference is this time. He was using me, a little old insignificant woman from Arkansas.

As I sat, He imparted more of His heart into me and poured out his instructions onto these pages. God revealed to me how this generation has become very grievous to God. He spoke with a resounding voice and said,

"THIS IS NOT MY CHURCH."

He sounded like a father who had suffered disappointment after disappointment with a child.

The church has become divided and distorted, and the prophets that could help have been put in exile. The false prophets masquerade before my people while attempting to shame the true prophets of God.

God calls the "true" prophets to come forth and denounce the false prophets, not just in word, but in deed. Integrity is being restored to the Office of the Prophet. No longer will people be able to masquerade as God's prophet. The prophets that are ascending in this dispensation are coming with power and authority. They will be unique and anointed with a fire that consumes the enemy. These prophets are rising to change the whole trajectory of the church.

Prophetic Inspiration

There will be times when you want to go beyond

what I tell you- DON'T

There will be times you want to prove them wrong and

prove who you are- DON'T

There are times when you will seem more human than

spirit- YOU'RE NOT

There will be times you feel so far from me-

KNOW I'M RIGHT HERE WITH YOU.

There will be times...

REMEMBER BECAUSE I AM, YOU ARE...

DESTINY CALLS!!!

Prophets Of Fire organization

Prophets of Fire was birthed from the desire to gather the prophets out of caves and exile, that they may come together and ignite a Holy Ghost fire in the land.

This fire is a consuming fire that consumes everything that is not like God and purifying fire, which will cleanse the body of Christ. The prophets shall go forth with power and authority, exercising dominion in the earth, with signs, wonders, and miracles.

www.ingramcontent.com/pod-product-compliance
Lightning Source LLC
Chambersburg PA
CBHW072156090426

42740CB00012B/2289